Original title:
A Jungle Beneath the Stairs

Copyright © 2025 Creative Arts Management OÜ
All rights reserved.

Author: Seraphina Caldwell
ISBN HARDBACK: 978-1-80581-859-5
ISBN PAPERBACK: 978-1-80581-386-6
ISBN EBOOK: 978-1-80581-859-5

Echoes of the Forgotten Green

Where the old shoes lie in pairs,
A ferret danced without any cares.
Lurking beneath the dusty wood,
Chasing after crumbs he found, he could.

A spider spun a web of glee,
It hummed a tune, oh so free.
The socks conspired in a heap,
Dreaming of adventures in their sleep.

The Lurking Wilderness Below

A sock puppet prince on his throne,
Declared the realm beneath his own.
He ruled with laughter, oh what fun,
As dust bunnies raced, and they could run.

The mice held court with tiny quips,
While crickets chirped their silly skips.
A parade of bugs in suits so neat,
Danced to the rhythm of tiny feet.

Shadows of the Wild

A shoe rack hid a wild affair,
With mismatched mates that had no care.
They whispered secrets of the day,
And giggled as they played away.

The fierce broom stood guard at night,
Chasing shadows, giving a fright.
But all the critters loved the game,
And chuckled loudly at the name.

Ferns and Fantasies Within

In the damp, dark space they thrived,
With ferns that twisted and arrived.
A bookworm's tale of daring plight,
As tales of ghosts took off in flight.

The tea party held by timid ants,
Wore hats of petals from curious plants.
Their laughter echoed through the night,
With whispers of whimsy, pure delight.

Secrets Blooming in the Dust

Tiny critters stomp and prance,
Dust bunnies lead a wild dance.
Socks and crumbs are treasures rare,
In this realm, none have a care.

Mice wear crowns of paper and glue,
Dancing in shoes they never knew.
Beneath the steps, a secret spree,
A merry band of oddity.

The Thriving Echo of Wilderness.

Underneath, a roach's parade,
Marches on with masquerade.
Limestone boulders, army ants,
Caterpillars in carrot pants.

Echoes of munching vibes abound,
The feast of crumbs grows rich and sound.
With laughter brewing in the air,
A banquet that all critters share.

Whispers of the Hidden Grove

In secret realms where shadows creep,
Fuzzy beetles softly leap.
Forget the silence of the night,
Funny squawks bring a jolly fright.

Beans and peas have joined the quest,
In this thicket, they jest and rest.
Where laughter blooms and echoes play,
A joyful forest hides away.

Secrets in the Shadows

Glimmers hide in corners deep,
Little beings in a heap.
Curling leaves like laughter fall,
Spinning tales within the hall.

Pillows made of crumpled fluff,
All declare they've had enough.
In shadows' dance and dust's embrace,
Life's a whimsical hiding place.

The Call of Hidden Life

Beneath the stairs, where shadows creep,
Tiny creatures dance in heaps.
A mouse dons shoes, a squirrel prances,
In this wild world, all take chances.

A rumble here, a squeak up there,
Secret parties, oh what a flair!
The dust bunnies serve, the ants hold court,
In this lively nook, all sorts cavort.

Secrets of the Shaded Hollow

In corners dark, secrets reside,
A toad sings tunes, the bugs coincide.
The cat pretends, it's all a show,
While raccoons share their prize catch below.

A pen cap fort, a paper plane,
Imaginations run wild, it's never plain.
Each creak of wood brings laughs anew,
In this hidden realm, mischief brews.

Spirits of the Forgotten Path

Along the edges where sunlight fades,
A lost sock laughs, its journey cascades.
Mice in top hats, they toast with cheese,
Their banter carried on the gentle breeze.

Pillows as clouds, with dreams to grow,
They sail on wishes, to and fro.
Invisible friends, they giggle and play,
In this whimsical path, all fears sway.

Fantasies in the Forgotten Cradle

A cradle sways, with stories untold,
Where teddy bears spin tales of old.
A dragonfly army on a mission to fly,
With unicorns joining the frolic nearby.

Bright paper boats in a puddle parade,
As giggles echo, they're never afraid.
With each tiny footstep, the fun does unfold,
In this cradle of dreams, adventure behold!

Chromatic Chronicles of the Underside

Colors clash and laughter spills,
Bright socks, mismatched, give us thrills.
Toys gather dust and secrets cheer,
Whispers tickle, magic is near.

Crayons roll in a jumbled spree,
Doodling dreams of what could be.
Lego castles, brave and wide,
Adventures lurch at every slide.

There's a cat with a regal air,
Painting portraits, slouched in glare.
Chasing shadows, what a race,
In this vibrant, hidden place.

Curiosities Underfoot

A rubber duck, a spongy shoe,
What mischief they must do!
Marbles play a sweet charade,
Clicking echoes never fade.

Old coins and buttons share their tales,
Worn-out socks with frayed details.
A treasure map made out of gum,
Leading to where the giggles come.

Tangled wires and lost delights,
Turn mundane into magic nights.
Every step, a chance to find,
The giggles left behind, unkind.

The Lush Haven

Underneath, where whispers loom,
Dreams sprout wild, dispelling gloom.
A plush giraffe strolls in delight,
Inviting all for a fun-filled night.

Cushioned vines twist and twirl,
As rainbows dance and colors swirl.
Conversations with a sock puppet sage,
Tell tales of the hidden page.

Beneath the stairs, joy takes flight,
In a kingdom built from sheer delight.
All are welcome, come and see,
The giggles burst with jubilee!

Hidden Footprints of Time

Footprints lead to places odd,
Where candy wrappers make a nod.
Forgotten cookies lie in wait,
For little hands to celebrate.

Whimsical paths of dust and cheer,
Map out stories we hold dear.
A lost ball bounces with a grin,
In this land where giggles begin.

Echoes of laughter fill the air,
Tickling toes without a care.
Join the parade, the fun is real,
In this treasure trove, we all feel.

The Veiled Wilderness

Under the stairs where shadows dwell,
Creatures play tricks, oh what a swell!
Rabbits with hats, and squirrels with ties,
Whispering secrets through giggles and sighs.

A cat in a crown, with a bustling parade,
Dances with mice, serenades are made.
Bouncing on cushions, a forest they find,
With chubby-cheeked bears that are silly and blind.

Hidden Realms of Magic

In the nooks, where dust bunnies leap,
A wizard's hat holds treasures to keep.
Butterflies chatter with ribbons of flair,
As shoes polish floors, pretending to care.

Lollipops grow on candy cane trees,
While teddies play chess with the buzzing bees.
The giggling spirits share tales of delight,
In the corners they twirl, from day into night.

Treasures in the Twisted Roots

Beneath the stairs, where the shadows twist,
A treasure map shows what can't be missed.
With candy coins and a gumball throne,
The whispered tales make the bravest groan.

In the bank of forgotten toys,
Dinosaurs dance, oh what a noise!
Goldfish in bowls throw bubbles around,
As offbeat melodies make silly sounds.

The Enchanted Underside

In the realm below where giggles ignite,
Goblins in slippers have parties all night.
They serve up snacks on a bananacake,
With fountains of soda, oh what a shake!

The walls are alive with stories to share,
While shadows spin tales of laughter and care.
A fairy with glasses recounts her mishaps,
As everyone joins in with playful claps.

Shadows Play Among the Stairs

In the corner where dust bunnies roam,
A critter in socks has made its home.
Squirrels wear ties and dance with flair,
In the shadows that tickle the stair.

Giggling mice hold a banquet grand,
With crumbs left behind by little hands.
They toast with acorns, sing with glee,
In a world where they rule, wild and free.

Adventures in the Hidden Layers

Under the landing, a kingdom grows,
Where the dust is thick and a faint breeze blows.
A raccoon in slippers gives quite a show,
With confetti made from paper and dough.

They sail on shoelaces, a daring crew,
Chasing the shadows, just me and you.
We giggle as we tumble, roll, then spin,
With every new stumble, the laughter begins.

The Lush Underfoot

What lies beneath in a world so vast?
Fuzzy mushrooms and laughter contrast.
Tiny frogs wear crowns of green,
Riding on beetles like kings of the scene.

Worms and snails throw a lively ball,
With guests very small, we're all having a ball.
Under the mat, where secrets dwell,
The wildest tales we have to tell.

Whispers of the Woodland Echo

In the shadows, the whispers flow,
As critters plot and scamper low.
A bear in pajamas reads tales of yore,
While raccoons play hide and seek at the floor.

Every squeak is a chuckle, every rustle a cheer,
As we peek through the spindles with giggles near.
There's mischief and magic behind every door,
As we join the fun in this world we adore.

The Resonant Peat

Beneath the creaks and groans of wood,
A world abuzz, misunderstood.
Tiny critters dance in pairs,
While socks and shoes hold secret stares.

The shadows chuckle, whispers sneak,
In dampened corners, giggles peak.
A toadstool throne where mischief reigns,
With frog choruses singing refrains.

Pine-scented trails of hidden quests,
Where dust bunnies fashion their vests.
Adventures bloom in curious spite,
A cardboard box turned spaceship flight.

And when the night steals the light away,
The whispers grow louder, come what may.
In this snug nook where wonders greet,
Life's funniest tales dance at our feet.

Life in the Underside

Under the stairs where shadows creep,
Gnomes wear hats, not meant for sleep.
The dustpan trolls hold court in glee,
As mismatched socks debate their spree.

A cobwebbed corner becomes a stage,
For beetle plays that seldom age.
The echoes of laughter drift on by,
While ants in tuxedos waltz and sigh.

In the quiet hum of hidden zest,
Bugs form teams for a game of chess.
A speckled rock, a mountain grand,
Where brave little critters make their stand.

And if you listen very close,
You'll hear them cheer for little Rose.
In this wild space, no grown-ups bide,
Life's a romp on the fun side.

Enchanted Echoes of the Hidden Trails

Beyond the clutter of everyday things,
A riddle of laughter, the spice that it brings.
Each shoe a tent, each bone an ode,
To a world where giggles forge the road.

The staircase hums a tune quite spry,
Where ladybugs drum under the sky.
A parade of crumbs, a feast unknown,
A grapevine tale, the seeds widely sown.

With a juggler's flair, the mice take flight,
On a journey planned for the deepening night.
And if you peek through a chip in the wall,
You might just spot the tallest of them all.

The echoes here sweetly tease the ear,
Molded from joy, sprinkled with cheer.
In this twinkling realm, full of quirks,
Life's a dance on the footsteps of work.

The Secret Life of Steps

Each step a story, a tale to tell,
Of mischief-makers and socks that fell.
In the spaces between, whispers and giggles,
As friendly spiders spin charming wiggles.

The baluster's beard hides whispers bold,
Where a squirrel tells tales of nuts, untold.
In this sneaky nook where no one can see,
A jester with acorns throws tea parties for free.

Rumble and tumble, the tumbleweeds spin,
With an orchestra of critters, ready to begin.
The echoes of fun ricochet and play,
As shadows peek out to seize the day.

So if you slip down when the lights go dim,
Join the raucous chants, embrace the whim.
For life's little secrets abound in delight,
In the land of the steps where all feels right.

Whispers of the Hidden Haven

In a spot not often seen,
Tiny critters dance with glee,
Emerald leaves and shadows lean,
A hidden world, just for me.

Frogs wear hats made from old socks,
While crickets tap in beetle bands,
Squirrels plot beneath the rocks,
With secret maps in tiny hands.

A raccoon juggles shiny things,
A parade of ants on a stroll,
Everyone laughs as laughter rings,
Underneath the wooden bowl.

Oh, the treasures that they hoard,
Marbles, buttons, and a shoe,
Life is fun, and never bored,
In this nook where mischief grew.

Secrets in the Shadowed Nook

Behind the stairs where no one peeks,
Live the bravest, wittiest mice,
With tiny scrolls and clever tweaks,
They plot their dreams, oh so nice!

A tiny mouse in cape and hat,
Leads a band of friends in play,
Telling tales of where they're at,
In their own, wild, mousey way.

They sneak away with crumbs of bread,
And cheese so rich, it makes them cheer,
A feast is laid on the floor, they said,
An applause from all who gather near.

So if you hear a little cheer,
From shadows where the dust bunnies sing,
Know the secret's drawing near,
In the nook, where laughter's king.

Roots of the Unseen Realm

Beneath the stairs, a kingdom grows,
Where boots and dust are out of place,
And plants in here wear funny clothes,
With roots that twist in a wild race.

Spiders weave their silky threads,
Beneath the wood, they laugh and spin,
While turtles claim their makeshift beds,
In this place where games begin.

An old shoe's a magic boat,
It sails through realms of dreams and fun,
With every laugh, the dreams will float,
As imaginary tales are spun.

So venture close, but do take care,
The voices here are quite a sight,
For in the roots, a world to share,
Awaits with giggles, day and night.

The Enchanted Underbelly

In a realm where dust bunnies play,
Magic lurks behind the frame,
Witches hold their tea parties, hey,
While goblins dance, calling your name.

Underneath, the socks are cars,
With teddy bears as drivers bold,
They ride through lands where laughter's stars,
Shine brightly, stories to be told.

And if you peek, don't startle them,
For they might throw a pillow fight,
With laughter ringing like a gem,
In the belly of the night.

So zip your lips, and tiptoe near,
Join the fun, just don't be loud,
For in this realm, oh have no fear,
The magic's waiting in a crowd.

Shadows in the Twilight Realm

In the corner lurks a beast,
With a belly rumbling loud,
It's just my cat, at least,
Not a monster from the crowd.

Dust bunnies dance, oh what a sight,
They twirl beneath the bed's soft glow,
With every rustle, they take flight,
In a world where wild things go.

A sock lays strewn, with stories grand,
Of adventures across the floor,
Where footsie battles take their stand,
It's chaos, laughter, evermore.

A shadow sneezes, what a fright!
I leap back with a goofy grin,
Who knew my closet held such bite,
With pillow fluff adorned within?

The Leafy Hideaway

Amidst faux plants and dust-stuffed things,
A squirrel's nest in a shoe for two,
With acorn snacks, it proudly brings,
A banquet fit for just a few.

The walls are shaky, but oh the glee,
As critters play their secret game,
With secret paths, a symphony,
Of giggles, chuckles, none to blame.

In corners hide some treasures rare,
Half a muffin, lost and free,
It's nature's feast, beyond compare,
A delightful mess for me to see.

So if you hear a creature's cheer,
Don't be alarmed, it's just a show,
In this leafy nook, so very near,
Where silliness and mischief grow.

The Chronicles of Damp Places

In the depths of shadows, tales are spun,
Of dust and damp, a grand parade,
With moldy bread and a rubber gun,
This realm of whimsy is well displayed.

A puddle forms, a mini lake,
Where fingers dip and giggles splash,
A rubber duck starts to partake,
In a carnival of water's crash.

Here rats wear hats and dance a jig,
As mice applaud, they take the stage,
Each step they take, a playful dig,
In chronicles of this damp age.

So join the fun, abandon fear,
The quirky quests beneath unfold,
With laughter ringing loud and clear,
In damp places, tales are told!

The Canopy of Secrets

Beneath the stairs, a world appears,
Where monsters hide and giggles sprout,
Behind the shadows, mixed up fears,
It's a kingdom of funny without a doubt.

A blanket fort, the castle grand,
Where noise and laughter intertwine,
Royalty in mismatched bands,
With secret paths in a world divine.

Crickets chirp their nighttime songs,
While pillows puff like clouds of fluff,
In this land where laughter throngs,
The canopy holds secrets, sure enough!

So if you stumble on this treasure,
With giggling gnomes and shadows bright,
Just settle in and share the pleasure,
In this hidden realm of pure delight!

The Life That Lurks Below

In shadows thick, the critters play,
A squirrel's rave, just out of sight.
They throw wild parties night and day,
While I just ponder, 'Is this right?'

I hear them giggling, what a scene,
With acorns flying through the air.
They've formed a band, the critter queen!
And who would think they'd have such flair!

A mouse doth dance upon a drum,
A beetle's solo steals the show.
I try to join but feel quite glum,
For they don't want a human foe!

So there I sit with snacks in hand,
Their laughter echoes, what a sound!
I wish I'd made a furry band,
To be a part of their shindig round.

Conundrum of the Overlooked Room

In the dusty corner, treasures lie,
Old shoes and toys from yesteryear.
A rubber duck might catch your eye,
But beware of what lurks near here!

I found a cat who wears a hat,
He claims he's king, doesn't like the mice.
They plot and scheme, it's quite the chat,
Why does my attic feel so nice?

A lizard plays a game of chess,
With a cockroach as his mate.
They've got a deal, I must confess,
To keep my secrets safe from fate.

Am I the guest, or am I host?
They throw a party, fill with cheer.
I sip my drink, I'm quite engrossed,
In this room of peculiar sphere.

The Mysterious Abode of Nature

Beneath the stairs, a world of green,
Where mushrooms dance and shadows creep.
A tiny gnome with broom so keen,
He's here to guard while we all sleep.

The plants gossip, oh what a sound,
About the lost socks, the dust bunnies.
They plot adventures, sneak around,
Making fun of our funny tummies.

A flower laughs, with petals bright,
It claims it's seen me trip and fall.
Oh, what a sight, it's all in spite,
But I'll just smile, I'm having a ball!

As I peek in, they all retreat,
With giggles soft, like whispers light.
I guess I'm not quite their heartbeat,
Just a visitor in their delight.

Forbidden Growth of the Basement

Beneath the steps, where dust is thick,
A garden blooms with socks and crumbs.
How did they grow? What a neat trick!
My laundry basket truly hums.

The spiders weave a tale of woe,
Their webs are homes, a bustling lab.
I saw a frog in pants, oh no!
Is this the life I want to grab?

Chasing a rat with a top hat on,
He's hosting tea with a sparrow guest.
They sip from cups, till break of dawn,
While I just sit, bemused but blessed.

Oh, dear basement, what a fine show,
Filled with antics and giggling crew.
I thought it dull, just walls and glow,
But here, the fun feels ever new!

Ferns and Fables

In the shadows of forgotten lands,
Little creatures tap their hands.
Whispers float on air so bright,
Telling tales till the morning light.

Giggling ferns dance with glee,
As silly bunnies sip herbal tea.
A squirrel in a hat, oh what a sight,
Claims he's the king, with acorns in flight.

Frogs croak songs of joyful cheer,
While mice in capes appear, oh dear!
Raccoons juggle nuts with flair,
In this leafy realm, without a care.

So tiptoe softly, laugh out loud,
Where every shadow wears a shroud.
In fables spun from vibrant greens,
Fun and mischief weave through scenes.

Adventures in the Dark Hollow

In a hollow where moonlight fails,
Critters plot in secret trails.
A hedgehog wears a tiny fork,
While owls dance and cats just stork.

Bats wear goggles, ready for flight,
Chasing fireflies, they spark delight.
The wise old turtle tells a joke,
That makes the shadows laugh and poke.

With every step, the ground might creak,
And underfoot, it giggles, squeaks.
Rabbits giggle 'round the bend,
As the night spills a playful blend.

So join the fun where laughter calls,
In this hollow of giggliest walls.
For every step holds a surprise,
In the land where laughter never dies.

The Kingdom of Forgotten Toys

Amidst the dust of yesteryear,
Lies a kingdom filled with cheer.
A doll with dreams who lost her hair,
Finds a bear who's quite debonair.

The toy soldiers march with pride,
While toy trains take a joyride.
A jack-in-the-box giggles loud,
As robots dance, all feeling proud.

Puzzles scatter across the floor,
Pieces chat, wanting more.
Kites that tease from high and low,
In this world, the strangest show.

So come and play with forgotten friends,
Where the fun and laughter never ends.
In their kingdom made of glee,
Childhood memories run wild and free!

Twilight in the Underfoot

When twilight whispers in the shade,
Little critters start their parade.
A snail wears glasses, quite a sight,
Reading poetry in the fading light.

The bugs all gather, spinning tales,
While hedgehogs in bow ties all sail.
Laughter bounces from root to root,
In the underfoot, the wise salute.

Mice are bakers, stirring treats,
While crickets play their jazzy beats.
In shadows deep, the mischief flows,
As the evening's magic brightly glows.

So stretch your ears, listen closely here,
In the twilight, there's nothing to fear.
With every giggle, your heart takes flight,
In the underfoot, oh what a night!

The Enchanted Corridor

In shadows lurk the critters small,
With tiny hats and a foot-high wall.
A raccoon in slippers, what a sight!
Doing the tango by the dim light.

The mice hold court with a kingly cheese,
Dancing around with the greatest of ease.
A squirrel with glasses reads aloud,
While the ants clap hands, they're really proud.

The old broom wiggles, it's got a flair,
As it sweeps away crumbs without a care.
The vacuum cleaner takes a break,
For even machines need time to shake!

Oh, what a world beneath our feet,
Where the wild and silly meet for a treat.
Next time you hear a ruckus below,
Just join the fun and put on a show!

Beneath the Forgotten Steps

In the gloom where shadows dance,
A pug in a tutu takes a chance.
He jigs and hops, the creatures cheer,
While a lizard dubs him the king of beer!

There's chatter and clamor, a furry brigade,
The elder hedgehogs join in the parade.
With vests made of leaves and ties snugly worn,
They toast to the day, each one a thorn.

A snail, with style, glides on a shell,
Stopping to gossip, 'Oh, do tell!'
While caterpillars knit with care,
Creating wild scarves for a winter rare.

In this realm of giggles and chatter loud,
The jungle of whimsy is always proud.
So if you hear a rumble or crash,
Just look below for the party bash!

Echoes of a Leafy Realm

Underneath where dust bunnies dwell,
Lies a critter club, oh, can't you tell?
A ferret recites Shakespeare with zest,
While the turtle gives fashion advice with a vest!

Vines hang low, like a curtain grand,
As frogs stage plays right on the sand.
An audience of beetles cheers with glee,
At the antics of critters, wild and free!

A squirrel dons shades, plays DJ with flair,
Spinning hits that dance through the air.
Amidst the chatter, a raccoon debates,
Whether pizza or pie makes for better plates.

So venture forth, hear the laughter rise,
In the hidden nook where the fun never dies.
Beneath your stairs, the show goes on,
The leafy land of giggles and brawn!

The Wilderness Within

In a nook where no one ever peeks,
A swashbuckling ferret takes daring leaps.
With a patchwork cape and a plastic sword,
He fights off dust balls, oh, they're bored!

A family of ants throws a surprise,
With tiny decorations to fill the skies.
They dance on crumbs, what a grand affair,
While a bird-watcher owl gives a wise glare.

A box turtle plays checkers, quite profound,
Against a wise rabbit, best in the round.
The stakes are high, a crumb of pie,
Oh, who will win beneath the sky?

So when you're down or feeling low,
Just peek beneath for a funny show.
With laughter echoing inside the walls,
Your imagination, it surely calls!

The Untamed Passageway

Under the steps, what lies in wait?
Whispers of dust, a curious state.
Mice in tuxedos dance on the floor,
As a dust bunny opens a tiny door.

Socks that went missing play hide and seek,
With a jazz band of crickets that never speak.
Lizards in sunglasses chill by the light,
While the old broom stirs up mischief by night.

Beneath the Stacked Memories

Old boxes pile high, a fortress of past,
A kingdom where laughter is meant to last.
A raccoon in a hat offers you tea,
Polka-dots on a parrot—come join me!

Under a blanket of forgotten dreams,
A world where nothing is quite what it seems.
The toys come alive as we giggle with glee,
In this quirky land, all are wild and free.

Serpents of the Wooden Threshold

Worms in tuxedos, slithering fast,
Chasing each other, a party amassed.
A caterpillar DJ spins tunes so bright,
While ants on parade groove all through the night.

The spiders are spinning a web of delight,
Hosting a ball under starlit bright light.
Laughter erupts, like bubbles in air,
As insects unite for the grandest affair.

Enigma of the Hidden Vines

Vines twist and turn in a playful dance,
Whispering secrets, giving chance a glance.
A frog in a bowtie croaks out a tune,
While turtles play poker beneath the full moon.

Chasing each other, the butterflies race,
In a dizzying swirl, they spin in a chase.
Under the thicket, a circus unfolds,
Where laughter is precious and never grows old.

Echoes of the Undergrowth

In a space where shadows play,
Little creatures scurry and sway,
A spare sock hangs like a vine,
Whispering secrets, oh so fine.

Dust bunnies bounce on tiny feet,
Pleased as punch in their secluded retreat,
With giggles hidden in the air,
Caught in their whimsical dare.

Forgotten toys join in the fun,
A long-lost doll, a toy gun run,
In this realm of fabricated cheer,
A laugh escapes—who's there to hear?

When mom comes down, they freeze in fright,
Hiding away from morning's light,
"Just a clutter," she shouts in despair,
As the echoes burst out—unaware.

The Mysterious Nook

In the corner, what's that smell?
A mystery wrapped, a hidden spell,
Old lunchbox, a crumbling roast,
The bravest critters love it most.

Mice don capes, play superhero,
While dusty spiders creep and grow,
Each morsel's treated like a prize,
Under the stairs, where magic lies.

A rubber band plays stretch and snap,
In this layer, they dance and clap,
With every twist and every turn,
The tales of wonder twist and churn.

When the door swings wide, they scatter fast,
The floor creaks loud, they're unsurpassed,
Yet in the shadows, laughter swells,
In the nook, where silence dwells.

Whimsy Amongst the Beams

Half-hidden, yet bold in their tricks,
Time ticks slowly, a space full of kicks,
A paper airplane flies with glee,
In this haven from reality.

Dust motes dance like fairies in flight,
As the glow of day turns into night,
With every squeak of creaky wood,
Silly imaginations spin the good.

Old magazines whisper tales of yore,
Kooky hairstyles that still adore,
Pet rats play drama in the gloom,
Transforming every corner to bloom.

When the laughter thunders like a storm,
The beams provide a comical form,
As we dive in, with no regrets,
Life's great prank, our loudest bets.

Beneath the Steps of Time

Where the odd socks keep their cheer,
And spiders dance with a wink, my dear,
The forgotten dust holds jokes untold,
Giggles weave through stories bold.

A shoe that lost its sole in fright,
Whispers secrets in the twilight light,
Tripping over stuffed toy dreams,
In this world where laughter beams.

Worn-out books with tales to share,
Of galactic squirrels and teddy bear flair,
As dust drifts down like confetti bright,
Each tale stirs laughter with delight.

So slip on shoes and join the dance,
In a kingdom where even shadows prance,
Among the layers of life, we roam,
In the place that most call home.

The Enigma of the Stairwell

In shadows deep, a secret waits,
With shoes and socks and stuffed-up mates.
A tiger made of dust bunnies prowls,
As giggles echo from the old woodowels.

Beneath the steps, the riddles thrive,
Where lost action figures come alive.
They plan their heist to steal the pie,
While squirrels plot and birds laugh high.

A tangled vine of tangled yarn,
Creeping forward, it brings alarm.
The cat stares down, a watchful king,
With minor thoughts of what treats will spring.

So tread with care, brave knobbly knees,
For adventures hide in creaks and wheezes.
Chart your course through socks and fluff,
You may just find you've had enough!

Musings of a Forgotten Vale

Once in a nook, where dust bunnies rise,
Lived a sock puppet with googly eyes.
He pondered if he might ever roam,
Past crumbs and shadows, far from home.

A pickle jar full of jellybeans,
Winked at the rat in his torn-up jeans.
Together they dreamed of lush green fields,
Where laughter blossomed and joy yields.

But the broom approached, a fierce foe near,
"Not today!" cried the puppet with cheer.
He fancied a dance, twirled round the floor,
And the rat joined in, they laughed evermore.

In that forgotten corner, alive with chatter,
Where socks make friends and trinkets splatter.
They'd toast their marshmallows on teacup flames,
In their wild little world, who cares for names!

Sagas in the Shade

Beneath the stairs, where sunbeams fall,
Lives a crew of critters, funny and small.
They swing on shoelaces, climb up rags,
With mischief in hearts and wagging tags.

A spider spins tales of heroic feats,
While ants serenade with their tiny beats.
Together they laugh, weaving gleeful threads,
As the mystery of lost cookies spreads.

A grumpy old box, filled with disdain,
Holds secrets of candy and long-lost fame.
Yet every day, he's a part of the play,
With critters declaring he's the king today.

So if you succumb to your tired old chair,
Remember the saga that lingers there.
Join in the fun, let imagination play,
For laughter is found in the silliest way!

The Forest of Whispering Echoes

A realm of giggles beneath the stair,
Where slippers dance and plush bears declare.
Each echo whispers tales of delight,
As the dust gathers stars and shines so bright.

A sock brigade marches in parade,
With mismatched uniforms, bold and unafraid.
They conquer the carpet, rise to the task,
And if you dare, you may join the masked.

A feathered friend chirps witty jests,
As tangled cords lay cozy nests.
The echo of laughter fills the domain,
In this odd little world, no one feels pain.

So step on softly, with wonder in mind,
Embrace the oddities you hope to find.
Let imagination soar, let your whims take flight,
In the secretive corners where joy ignites!

Life Among the Dusty Steps

Under the stairs, the dust bunnies play,
They bounce and they tumble, oh what a display!
A sock puppet army leads the parade,
While a rogue shoe joins, a new friend is made.

The spider's a jester, making us laugh,
With webs that shimmer and never feel half.
A rumble of laughter from the stale air,
As someone trips lightly, unaware of the dare.

Old boxes keep secrets, a forgotten past,
A rubber chicken quacks, what a delight to cast!
The mice hold their meetings, plotting a snack,
While a cat peeks in, with one sneaky paw back.

So here in this corner, such joy can be found,
In the tickling shadows, we're awfully sound.
With giggles and squeaks, it's a raucous affair,
Life's oddly amusing, when lived unaware.

Mysteries in the Darkened Corner

In the darkened corner, oh what do I see?
A gnome with a hat, sipping fine herbal tea.
He winks and he guffaws, with twinkling delight,
As the shadows grow thicker, we bathe in moonlight.

A hidden treasure – a dust-covered shoe,
Perhaps once a hero, now lost to the crew.
With cobwebs like curtains, the secrets unfold,
In this world of mischief, the stories are bold.

A distant echo calls, it's a cricket that sings,
Of adventures long past, and strange little things.
The chew toy's a king, and beneath him, popcorn,
With laughter that rolls in the breeze of the morn.

So venture on softly, come witness the cheer,
In this mysterious corner, amusement is near.
For every dark spot hid, a giggle does bloom,
Where whimsy and wonder erase every gloom.

Adventure in the Sweet Sepulcher

In the sweet sepulcher, where whispers abound,
The echoes of laughter, they dance all around.
A toy dinosaur guards the chocolate stash,
While gummy bears trade secrets in a flash.

A treasure map drawn on an old pizza box,
Leads to the land of abandoned socks.
We trek over teddies, through mazes of plush,
As the grand adventure ignites quite a rush.

But beware of the broom, it's alive with a swish,
It'll sweep you up fast, oh, do not be a dish!
The dust mites are pirates, their ship's made of crumbs,
Ready to board, they'll take you for funs!

So let's sail through the giggles, and bask in the flair,
For each little moment, we breathe in the air.
In this sugary fortress, our laughter's the gain,
In sweet sepulchers, we'll always remain.

Tales from Under the House

Under the house, where the shadows conspire,
Lies a kingdom of wonder, set hearts all afire.
A lizard in glasses, he reads the news page,
While shadows of nightmares tap dance on a stage.

The old wooden beams, they creak as they smile,
With memories of creatures that linger a while.
A family of mice run a funny old show,
While sneakers and sandals join in for the glow.

Beneath ancient floors, a party begins,
With slapstick and gags, it's where laughter spins.
A jack-in-the-box springs forth with a shout,
And advises us all to never feel doubt!

So gather your courage, come join in the fun,
For tales from this realm have just just begun.
With chuckles and giggles, we'll dwell in delight,
In the laughter that blooms when the shadows are bright.

Treasures of the Forgotten Den

A sock with stripes, a shoe with flair,
A rubber duck just hanging there.
A treasure chest with dust and grime,
My mighty haul, a lovely find!

A squashed-up snack, once full of cheer,
A toy that's lost its squeak, oh dear!
With giggles loud, I gather all,
In this secret space, I heed the call.

Adventures hide in every nook,
Each forgotten thing a storybook.
With every rummage, joy I feel,
In this strange realm, it's all surreal.

So here I sit, my kingdom grand,
Among lost treasures, dreams so planned.
While dust bunnies dance a silly jig,
I reign supreme, a mighty fig!

The Wild Where No Light Reaches

In darkened corners, shadows stray,
A monster's roar? Nah, just a stray.
It munches on the crumbs I left,
A friendly beast? Why, I am bereft!

A lion's mane? No, just some fluff,
A trail of toys makes it quite tough.
I step with care through bramble and mess,
Searching for fun, not needing a dress.

Tigers peek from out of sight,
Barking dogs join in the fright.
But in this wild where giggles roar,
I find my heart's true treasure store.

Each rustle brings a chuckle near,
A pouncing cat? No, just my gear.
Together we'll weave a great grand tale,
Of furry paws and silly trails!

Whispers Between the Beams

Here lie secrets, whispers shared,
Invisible friends, forever spared.
A tickle from a passing breeze,
Laughter rings like chimes through trees.

The beams above can hear it all,
Dreams big and small, in hardwood hall.
A squirrel's chatter, a spider's spin,
In this space, mischief begins.

With tick-tock clocks and shadows flit,
Each creaky board just adds to wit.
Beneath the stairs, where giggles sing,
A secret world, oh what a thing!

The house creaks low, a giggling sound,
In a land of whispers, joy is found.
With every rustling, hearts do soar,
In this playful realm, forevermore!

A Green Symphony in the Gloom

Under the stairs, where shadows play,
Fern fronds sway in a ballet.
Laughter bubbles like a brook,
In this green world, take a look!

A pixie stomping on a leaf,
Dancing freely, sheer belief.
Mossy paths of silvery sheen,
In the gloom, we reign the green.

Each twig a wand, a magic tease,
Spinning webs with playful ease.
Leaves can whisper, trees can hum,
In this zany realm, we have fun.

So come along, let's venture down,
With giggles loud, we'll own this town.
In forgotten realms, where shadows play,
A wild parade, we'll lead the way!

Enigmas of the Lower Realm

In the shadows, rustles play,
Tiny creatures laugh and sway.
A sock parade, they march around,
Beneath the steps, a world is found.

A mouse with boots, a squirrel with flair,
Debates of cheese float through the air.
With acorn caps as tiny hats,
All's a circus with furry chitchats.

A peek-a-boo game from underneath,
Whispers of mischief, spoilers bequeath.
Toys long lost, now spark their glee,
Seeking treasure, a friendly spree.

With giggles and giggles, the fun ignites,
Beneath our feet, life's merry frights.
In this funny realm, they live with zest,
Who knew such joy could hide and rest?

The Whispering Embers

In the corner where dust bunnies reside,
Flickering tales of sparks collide.
Crumbs exchanged for secrets rare,
Cinnamon whispers blend in the air.

A matchstick giraffe, a paperclip man,
Playing hide-and-seek from a tiny fan.
Every glow tells a tale so strange,
In the low-lit nook where shadows range.

The chatter of crumbs, a rustling cheer,
A symphony thrives, though no one's near.
With giggles and glee, they dance on their toes,
In their realm, anything goes!

So next time you hear a rustle or hum,
Know there's magic, where life is fun.
Amidst the quiet, a party's begun,
In the corners, joy's never done.

The Wandering Shadows

Beneath the steps where mauve meets gray,
Shadows wander and play all day.
Underwear puppets put on a show,
With floppy feet, they steal the glow.

A wobbly figure, a flashlight knight,
Defending the crumbs from the looming night.
With squeaky voices, they share their tales,
Of pizza adventures and wonderful fails.

Tangles of laughter echo in grooves,
While goofball spectres create their moves.
A sassy sock sings a silly song,
In their hidden world, they all belong.

So if you hear a chuckle or cheer,
Don't be alarmed, it's just their cheer.
In the space where giggles scout,
Their sneaky shenanigans dance about.

Fables of the Sunken Earth

Under the steps, where oddities thrive,
Stories unfold, keeping dreams alive.
Tin cans chatter, a dialogue bright,
As misfit toys bask in the light.

A rubber duck spins tales of the sea,
While tattered bears plot a mighty spree.
In this realm of laughter and cheer,
Every lost item becomes a souvenir.

Old batteries chant their electrifying lore,
At scavenger hunts, they all implore.
With giggles aplenty, they navigate,
In this secret domain, they celebrate.

So listen close when you climb the stairs,
For wondrous fables weave through the air.
In the sunken world, a laughter surge,
Where every oddity sings and merges.

Underworld of Dreams

In the shadows, creatures prance,
Socks and shoes, they hold a dance.
A sandwich lost, a crumb or two,
They feast on snacks, oh what a view!

They play hide and seek with dust,
In the corners, wanderlust.
A rogue toy train zooms around,
In this realm, fun knows no bounds.

With giggles and munchies, they thrive,
As the dust bunnies come alive.
Whispers float, a secret crew,
In this land where dreams come true!

The clock ticks loud, but they don't care,
Time is a joke; they're unaware.
Underneath, they dance and play,
In their wild and whacky way!

The Canopy of Memories

Beneath the stairs, a world appears,
With shoes and books and forgotten years.
Where monsters lurk and giggles rise,
A wild kingdom in disguise!

Fluffy cushions hold the throne,
Snacks and sips, but they're all alone.
A treasure map made of old tape,
Sending adventurers on a shape!

Tangled strings of thoughts unwind,
Each twist and turn is one of a kind.
Whirly giggles, toys take flight,
In this cozy realm, all feels right!

With a squeaky voice, the teddy speaks,
Sharing secrets as the clock ticks weeks.
In the quiet, joy ignites,
In this nook, pure delight!

Fantasies in the Land of Dust

Dust motes dance like fairy sprites,
When the house sleeps, they claim the nights.
Cracked crayons sketch a world so bright,
Where everything's just out of sight!

A brave cat sets out on a quest,
To find the toy that's long been stressed.
A sock monster, giggling with glee,
Unraveling mischief, oh can't you see?

With marshmallow clouds and gumdrop trees,
Imagination runs free on a breeze.
Each corner hides treasure galore,
Lurking shy, behind the old door!

Grand tales spun from the fabric of dreams,
With marshmallow peeps and candy streams.
In this land where silliness reigns,
Every moment's full of joyful gains!

Nature's Forgotten Stage

A cluttered space where laughter lives,
The old shoes preach what nonsense gives.
Crayons stand as mighty trees,
With giggles echoing in the breeze!

Dinosaur socks take center stage,
In this wild, imagin'd page.
In the shadow, a sandwich waits,
For jungle beasts with grand debates!

An orchestra of dust bunnies plays,
With rhythms that dance through cloudy haze.
Squeaky voices join the sound,
In this magical mess that knows no bounds!

So here we sit, with laughter high,
With visions that soar as we take to the sky.
In this playhouse made of dreams,
Life is sillier than it seems!

Stories from the Dusty Depths

In a nook where shoes reside,
A world of critters tries to hide.
Socks become their cozy caves,
In dusty lands, they brave the waves.

With tiny hats made from a sock,
The mice all dance and laugh and mock.
Their cheese plates served on shiny tiles,
They toast to life with squeaky smiles.

Dust bunnies bounce with joyful glee,
While spiders weave a tapestry.
Lost toys tell tales of days gone past,
In this maze, the fun is vast.

So next time when you climb upstairs,
Listen close to their playful wares.
For beneath your feet, dear friend,
Laughter thrives, and joy won't end.

The Secret Garden of Shadows

Behind the wood where dust collects,
A playful band of shadows flex.
They bloom like flowers in the night,
With giggles growing pure delight.

A spoonful of mischief in the air,
They leap and dance without a care.
The old yarn tangled up with cheer,
In shadowed bounds, there's naught to fear.

Each corner hosts a playful plot,
With tiny gnomes who giggle a lot.
Their leafy hats a sign of fun,
Playing games till day is done.

So tiptoe softly, come and see,
Where giggles sprout from harmony.
A secret realm beneath the light,
A whimsical show, oh what a sight!

Creatures of the Subterranean Realm

In deep dark corners, they convene,
With silly hats and eyes that glean.
A tangle of laundry is their land,
Their ruler is a laughing band.

With rubber ducks and crumbs galore,
They host their feast behind the door.
The old broom whispers tales of yore,
As they dance and sing, and ask for more.

A jester beetle cracks a joke,
While tired shoes become their cloak.
From hidden spots, they peek and plot,
Finding joy in every thought.

So if you hear a chuckle low,
Or see a shadow flit and flow,
Just know there's fun beneath your feet,
Where creatures dwell and laughter meets.

Tales from the Crumbling Staircase

On the stairs where dust bunnies roam,
A family of ants calls it home.
They march in line with snacks to share,
Their little picnic fill the air.

A cat with dreams of soaring high,
Plots mischief with a glittering eye.
With a pounce and swish, he tries to tease,
But the ants just giggle with perfect ease.

The steps hold stories untold and bright,
From shadows that dance in the moonlight.
With each creak and groan, a secret's spun,
In the world below, the antics run.

So listen close to the staircase sound,
For the whispers of laughter can surely be found.
In the currents of dust, the tales take wing,
Where the heart of the staircase lets happiness sing.

The Lurking Canopy

Beneath the drapes, a creature stirs,
A tangled web of giggles purrs.
A squirrel with socks, a lion in shades,
Hosting a party in leafy cascades.

Plates of acorns and cups of dew,
Uncle Toad brings a cracking brew.
They dance around, with flailing arms,
To tunes of whimsy, away from harms.

Upon a branch, two parrots squawk,
While a raccoon tries to learn to walk.
The chandelier swings, candles ablaze,
Decorating chaos in zany malaise.

So if you peek, don't grab your phone,
Join in the laughter from wood and stone.
For secret life thrives, just out of sight,
In the cozy nook, where critters delight.

Steps to a Wild Domain

Every creak brings a muted cheer,
As critters gather, no need to fear.
The stairs are alive, with whispers and glee,
Of dances and games, come take a peek!

A tortoise races a mouse on a hill,
While bugs join in, with skips and shrill.
Over the carpet, they chase and play,
In their wild world, where rules melt away.

A parrot critiques the moonlit glow,
Claiming it shines like a game show.
With feathers afluff, and sass in the air,
They toast with tea, and laughter to share.

When night creeps in, adventures are plenty,
With tales running wild, and nonsense aplenty.
So tiptoe softly, embrace the thrill,
Join the ruckus, and laugh until.

Beneath the Wooden Veil

Under a scarred and creaky slab,
Lies a realm with secrets to grab.
A hedgehog laughs at the squirrel's hat,
While planning a prank on a sleepy cat.

The dust bunnies hold a secret show,
With acorn caps as hats aglow.
In a cardboard box, the fun unfolds,
Tales of adventure, wildly told.

A fuzzball sings with a voice of cheese,
The audience roars, all down on their knees.
They cheer and shout, for more to come,
As the clock strikes ten, the ruckus hums.

So come on down, when shadows play,
In this quaint nook where creatures sway.
With giggles and grins, their hearts entwined,
In the merry chaos, true joy you'll find.

The Mythical Burrow

In a hollow below, where shadows clash,
A rabbit plans a dash for a stash.
With carrots piled high, a feast to deploy,
He dreams of a realm that sings with joy.

A lizard jives in a leaping spree,
Dancing in circles, all wild and free.
The lantern bugs buzz, in a shining array,
Lighting the night, guiding the play.

An owl hoots loudly, deciding to preach,
While a rabbit rolls his eyes, out of reach.
"Who needs the wisdom when jokes are around?
In this burrow of fun, it's laughter we've found!"

So if you stumble on this hidden lair,
Just know the giggles waft through the air.
Join the escape to the land of delight,
Where mischief rules until the first light.

Tales of the Hidden Oasis

In the gloom where dust bunnies play,
A frog wears a hat, shouts, "Hip-hip-hooray!"
Cockroaches throw parties, oh what a sight,
They dance with the crumbs 'til the morning light.

Lost socks form a band, they groove with glee,
While spiders serve tea, oh such mystery!
With pillows for mountains and blankets for seas,
Adventure unfolds with the slightest of breeze.

The rubber duck sits, a king on his throne,
Quacking for all, he's never alone.
The dust settles softly as the giggles rise,
A kingdom of laughter under the skies.

But when the footfalls stomp, all hustle and rush,
The critters all freeze, in a fervent hush.
When silence returns, out they come again,
To wriggle and dance with the joining of friends.

The Awakened Roots

Beneath the steps where no one dares peek,
Roots stretch and yawn, feeling quite unique.
They whisper to each other, gossip galore,
About the dust mites that visit and snore.

A cricket dons glasses, reads tales from a shoe,
Sipping on dew in the morning hue.
He offers sage wisdom, "Don't fear the shoe print!"
While centipedes nod, sharing a light hint.

The caterpillars host a daytime rave,
Swinging from shoelaces, feeling quite brave.
Pockets of sunlight filter through the cracks,
While the shadows all wink, no need to relax!

If you listen real close, you'll hear their retreat,
Saying goodnight with a soft, gentle beat.
As the world above turns into a blur,
They plan a parade, oh, the tales they confer!

Below the Surface of Shadows

In the cracks of the floor, where secrets abide,
A family of mice takes an amusing ride.
They hitch on a crumb, sail down to the end,
While the shadows all giggle, they play with no bend.

A battle ensues with old paper clips,
The raccoons use them for interesting trips.
They launch to the skies, oh what a delight,
With a flick of a tail, they disappear from sight.

The dusty old boots are an elephant's lair,
Where choppy discussions bring forth such a flair.
They argue and chuckle about who is the best,
As the spiders spin tales on the tops of their nests.

But when the clock strikes, all games must ensue,
The critters scatter, just a brief adieu.
Hidden from eyes, they giggle with glee,
For tomorrow will bring more fun, can't you see?

Intricacies of the Hidden Grove

In the shadows between a sandwich and gum,
Lies a pancake house where the ants all come.
They flip little cakes on a matchstick grill,
With syrupy laughter, it's quite the thrill.

The beetles are baristas, whirling around,
Creating a coffee that's truly renowned.
With twigs for the stirrers and leaves for the cups,
They sip on sweet dreams as the sun comes up.

Worms gather 'round for a game of charades,
While fairy dust flitters and softly cascades.
Chasing the twinkling like fireflies in flight,
Each moment's a treasure, a whimsical sight.

But when the sunlight casts long shadows anew,
The giggles grow quiet, and they bid adieu.
For in the small nooks where fun quickly flows,
Night brings the magic that only one knows.

Secrets of the Petal-Laden Floor

In the corner, blooms aglow,
A flower's dance, a secret show.
The dust bunnies twist and twirl,
A petal party, nature's whirl.

A cheeky beetle dons a hat,
While ants hold court, they chat and spat.
In this realm of vibrant cheer,
The floor's a stage, let's make it clear!

A worm recites his wiggly rhyme,
The clock ticks on, but who has time?
With giggles shared and snacks galore,
Life blooms bright on the petal floor.

When guests arrive, they stumble wide,
Unseen parties where critters reside.
Shhh! Don't tell them, it's our quest,
To live like plants, we're simply blessed!

The Realm of Crinkled Leaves

In the shadow, life awaits,
Crinkled leaves make funny plates.
A snail rehearses its slow ballet,
While mushrooms giggle in dismay.

Squirrels plot a heist for crumbs,
While lizards hum out silly drums.
A breeze whips by, the leaves take flight,
In this realm, it's pure delight.

An old shoe's home for a frog or two,
With whispers shared, and giggles too.
Laughter echoes through each nook,
In the crinkles, magic's hook.

Listen close, do you hear that sound?
The crunch of fun all around!
Nature's jesters, bold and spry,
In the realm, let joy fly high!

Beneath the Echoing Arch

Underneath the creaky stair,
Echoes dance with lively flair.
A spider spins a web of fun,
Where laughter lingers, never done.

Dust motes swirl, a twinkling show,
As shadows play and tease below.
A cat leaps high with a startled yowl,
In this playhouse, even mice howl!

Cocoa spills and giggles ring,
Every nook a secret spring.
With phantoms of socks lost before,
This archway holds a merry lore.

So if you hear some chuckles near,
Know it's just the party here.
Join the fun, don't miss the mark,
It's a wild bash beneath the arc!

Life Within the Cracks

In the crevices, life does creep,
Where tiny critters dream and leap.
A mouse with flair, a stout raccoon,
Hold court by fading light of noon.

A family of ants makes quite a fuss,
While a sleepy spider rides a bus.
In this world of giggles and mess,
Every crack's a fun express!

Penny treasures left behind,
Turn to crowns for creepies kind.
With rumbles of laughter, tales are told,
In every chip and wrinkle of old.

Watch your step and keep it light,
For beneath our feet, a perfect sight.
Life's a party in each little crack,
Join the fun, there's no turning back!

www.ingramcontent.com/pod-product-compliance
Lightning Source LLC
Chambersburg PA
CBHW070311120526
44590CB00017B/2626